MEDITATIONS ON THE PASSION

P9-DBT-082

MEDITATIONS ON THE PASSION
Two Meditations on Mark 8:31– 38

Johann Baptist Metz and Jürgen Moltmann

translated by
Edmund Colledge

Paulist Press
New York/Ramsey/Toronto

First published in German in 1974, copyright © 1974 by Verlag Herder KG Freiburg im Breisgau.

English translation, copyright © 1979 by The Missionary Society of St. Paul the Apostle in the State of New York

All rights reserved. No part of this book may be reproduced or transmitted in any form or by any means, electronic or mechanical, including photocopying, recording or by any information storage and retrieval system without permission in writing from the Publisher.

Library of Congress
Catalog Card Number: 78-70823

ISBN: 0-8091-2184-0

Published by Paulist Press
Editorial Office: 1865 Broadway, New York, N.Y. 10023
Business Office: 545 Island Road, Ramsey, N.J. 07446

Printed and bound in the
United States of America

Contents

Foreword

These two meditations on Mark 8:31—38 were originally delivered at the Fifteenth Congress of the German Evangelical Church in Düsseldorf; and at that time they were coordinated, so as to put into words our common response to the demands of the text. Also, our consideration of 'The Story of the Passion' enabled us to state what we agree in considering important and shared in our theological work. So we have been glad to accede to the wish that both our texts might appear in a single publication.

Fall 1973   J.B.Metz - J.Moltmann.

I

The Passion of the Son of Man and His Call to follow Him

———————◆———————

Jürgen Moltmann

Mark 8:31 — 38 (1)

First Announcement of the Passion
& The Call to Follow Jesus

————————◆————————

31 And he began to teach them: 'The Son of Man must suffer many things, and be rejected by the elders, the high priests and the learned scribes, and be put to death, and after three days rise again.'

32 And he said this openly. But Peter took him on one side and began to reprehend him. 33 But he turned around and looked at his disciples and reprehended Peter and said: 'Go back and leave me, you Satan; for you are thinking the thoughts not of God but of men'.

34 And he called the people to him together with his disciples and said to them: 'If anyone wishes to follow after me, then let him deny himself and take his cross upon him and follow me. 35 For whoever wishes to save his life will lose it; but whoever loses his life for the sake of me and of the Gospel will save it.

36 For what will it help a man to gain the whole world and forfeit his life?

37 For what could a man pay as a price for his life? 38 For whoever is ashamed of me and of my words in this adulterous and sinful generation, the Son of Man will be ashamed of him, when he comes in the glory of his Father with the holy angels'.

1

The Secret of Jesus
and his Revelation in Suffering

———◆———

This text is called 'Jesus's first proclamation of his Passion'. It includes his call to us to follow him. The text comes almost in the middle of Mark's Gospel, after Jesus's miracles and parables and before his journey to death on the Cross upon Golgotha.

It is preceded by the miracle in which a blind man is given sight, so that people think that Jesus is John the Baptist, Elias or some other resurrected prophet of the past.

It is preceded by Jesus's open question to the disciples: 'And who do you say that I am?'

Peter confesses him as the 'Christ', that is, the liberator of Israel, the Messias of the last days. Jesus reprehends this confession. No-one must know it. Jesus's own answer to the question, who in fact is he? Is his way towards suffering, rejection and death. It is only this way which reveals his secret. His end upon the Cross tells who in truth he is.

So at the same time it becomes a serious matter for all who listen to him. Until then the disciples had watched miracles and listened to parables. Until then they had gone at his side, with their own notions and dreams about him and about their future. But now they are called to follow him and drawn into his way. They will recognize in his sufferings who he is, and his sufferings upon the Cross will shatter their wishful dreams. They will serve life and find life by following him in their own sufferings, and the realities of this life will fundamentally change their notions about life.

Both sections of this text are inseparably related:

• We cannot follow Jesus in suffering without confessing and assenting to the suffering, rejected and crucified Son of Man.

• We cannot confess this Son of Man without denying ourselves and surrendering to the suffering which redeems the world.

Whoever understands the suffering of the Son of Man has understood God.

Whoever takes his cross upon himself and follows him will find life.

2

The Way of Suffering of the Son of Man in the World's Inhumanity to Man

---◆◆---

'The Son of Man must suffer many things, and be rejected by the elders, the high priests and the learned scribes, and be put to death, and after three days rise again'.

Jesus here recounts his sufferings in an ascending order:

-suffering

-rejection

-death.

What do these mean?

Suffering here means: to be maltreated by men, to encounter their resistance, to accept their contradiction and to be brought down by one's adversaries. 'To suffer many things' means: to suffer immeasurably and interminably, and without inner resistance and outward defence. Whenever one man suffers, there is on the other hand aggression, hatred and evil. These things, as we know, are born of fear. Men let someone else atone for what oppresses them. They look for a scapegoat on to which they can thrust their own self-hatred. They pass on their own sufferings to others, and allow them to suffer.

Suffering and letting suffer, fear and aggression make

our world so intolerable, make it inhuman. That is why the 'Son of Man' must suffer many things.

To be rejected is not the same, but a higher degree of suffering. Suffering can be borne with dignity. One must have compassion for the suffering. One should respect those who show great patience. Even Israel often martyred its prophets. In an unjust world 'the just man must suffer much', they say. But one who is rejected cannot be a prophet of God and a just man. Indeed, he is rejected in God's name as godless, in the name of the holy Law as a lawbreaker. Rejection robs this suffering man of every dignity. His suffering has no honour. There is no room here for compassion. To suffer as one rejected means that one must die crying out 'My God, why have you forsaken me?' Whoever so suffers and dies experiences a total dereliction. By human standards he enters comfortless into the 'death of God', into the absolute death of forsakenness.

The *death* which Jesus sees ahead of him will mean that he must endure mankind's sufferings, turned against him and thrust upon him, that he must endure rejection by God and his Law; and he accepts it as the divine will for the sake of man.

That is why he foretells that he will 'after three days be reawakened', not with a resounding 'but', instead, with a quiet 'and'. Whoever knows and experiences suffering and the meaning of contempt and rejection cannot regard that as a 'happy end' which will put everything right again; rather, it is a tremendous surprise. God reawakens a suffering man; that is imaginable, if he was of exemplary justice. God reawakens one who had been rejected; either this is impossible, or it is something completely new. It is impossible, if God guarantees the way of this world, with its laws and its retributions. It is something completely new, if in the suffering and death of this Son of Man, God and his will are revealed, and set aside this world and its ways so that the Son of Man's rule over men may conquer. If he is 'reawakened after three days', there will be revealed to us freedom through this man's suffering, grace through this man's rejection, eternal life through this man's death, and God's humanity through this man's divinity.

Who is the *Son of Man*? In contrast to Peter's very direct attribution to Jesus of the title 'Christ', Jesus here is speaking of himself extremely indirectly, as he speaks of the mission and the fate of the 'Son of Man'. He is speaking of the 'Son of Man' as if this were a personality into which he has only now grown, a future upon which he has only now entered. The earthly Jesus manifestly lives for what he will become. Only his end upon the Cross and his resurrection will reveal who in truth he is. That is why a 'Messianic mystery' is imposed upon his way of life: his words, his deeds and his sufferings are determined by what will be revealed as the uniqueness of his being.

According to chapter 7 of Daniel, the 'Son of Man' may be the true Israel, according to Jewish apocalyptic writings he may be the judge of the universe who is to come, according to Ezechiel he may be God's prophet. None of these three concepts, formed from the hopes of

Israel, correspond — or, at most, partially only — with Jesus. He never identifies himself with one of these manifestations of the peoples' hopes as they recalled the Old Testament. So we must understand through Jesus the title 'Son of Man', and not through the title understand Jesus. *Jesus, the Son of Man*, means (however much Rudolf Augstein may doubt this) *Ecce Homo*; behold the true man in an inhuman world. *Jesus the Son of Man* also means at one and the same time: *Ecce Deus*: behold the true God in a world of evil spirits and false gods.

Thus, whoever understands this Son of Man has understood God.

Whoever wants to comprehend God must, paradoxically, look upon this Son of Man in his suffering.

'The Son of Man *must* suffer many things . . .'

This *must* expresses his divine destiny. It is a 'must' which God has promised, a promise which demands fulfilment. But because he must, no tragic destiny is imposed on him. He is not following Oedipus's dark fate or Socrates's friendly guardian spirit. He is following the will of the God whom he so confidently calls 'my Father'. It is because this is no predetermined and inescapable fate that Jesus from the beginning found his life one continuous temptation to avoid the demands of that fatherly will and the fulfilment of that divine promise, a temptation not to drink the 'cup of suffering', as it is called. But he cannot spare himself this 'must', and, what is more, he cannot spare the men who will torment and reject and kill him from his suffering and rejection and death. Therefore every invitation to turn aside from this path appears to him as Satanic.

That makes clear the *story of Peter* which follows. Just now, Peter was the one confessing Christ. Now he is the one denying that Jesus must suffer. He even reprehends Jesus, and his remonstrance is a passionate entreaty. We do not know what was in Peter's mind. Was his ideal of Christ one of power politics, all glory and prestige, which must not suffer? Was it human suffering? In studied fashion Jesus turns away from Peter and to the disciples: it is the work of Satan to oppose the will of God, to want to impede Jesus on his way of suffering, and so to do just what all men want. And, by contrast, it is divine to do as the Son of Man should do and wants to do, to take upon oneself to suffer many things and to bear rejection and to die.

The sharpness of the contrast is extraordinary; what is averagely human, all too human, is Satanic; and what is divine is truly human, the way of the Son of Man. The decision between them challenges Jesus's person and his way.

Peter wants what all men want. What is it, in this respect, that all men want? They love strength, power, success. We want to achieve. We want to be immune from frustration, suffering and contempt. That is why many compensate for their uncertainties with omnipotent fantasies, and look for strong men and ideologies of power. It is only power which impresses. It is only success which succeeds. Therefore, those who idolize power, honours and success must not suffer.

But the Son of Man is subject to divine necessity, not to this all too human and yet Satanic compulsion. He can suffer, and he wants to endure the contradiction of the inhuman so as to rescue it from its inhumanity. He can be rejected, and he wants to be rejected, so as to take away inhumanity's rejection. He can be forsaken by God, his Father, and he wants to bear forsakenness by God, to drive it from the world. Why can he do all this, and why does he want all this? He can do it, because he is plainly free of that fear which cannot want to do it. He can do it, because he is free of that guilt which must always turn aggressive. He can do it, because he does not succumb to Satan's temptation to idolize himself and despise what in him is human. Precisely in this does he manifest himself as the 'Son of Man' that he makes himself so vulnerable to rejection and death. Only God can do that, and only God wants that. For God is God and is free precisely because he permits himself, in his Son of Man, to be so wounded and despised and slain.

It is from this confrontation that the altercation between Peter and Jesus proceeds.

There is the *man wishing to be God*, fleeing suffering, guilt and fear, pursuing honours and a life of bliss — and here is the *God who is man*, taking upon himself man's despised and vulnerable humanity and permitting himself to be humiliated.

There is the *man fighting his way up*, who wants his gods and ideals to be impassible, powerful, victorious, promising success — and here is the suffering, swooning and

12

crucified God who loves his people as they truly are: uncertain, mortal, at each other's mercy. It is the confrontation between the *all too human Satan*, dehumanizing men because he promises them a divinity which they cannot bear, and *God's Son of Man*, making men human by taking upon himself their inhumanity.

Whoever sees the suffering of the Son of Man sees God in an inhuman world.

He does not see the god of men's dreams, all glory and prestige, but the true, the free, the loving and human God. This recognition does indeed destroy the notions of godlike greatness which men perversely chase. But it brings despised humanity.

3

Following the Way of the Cross

───────◆◆───────

The text continues: '*And he called the people to him with his disciples and said: If anyone wants to follow me. . .*' This is a remarkable transition: now Jesus calls 'the people' to him and only includes his disciples in his discourse, which is addressed to all and sundry. '*If* anyone wants to follow me . . .' No-one is compelled to go this way. Jesus does not expect even his disciples to follow him in suffering. What he proposes is so drastic that it must be every man's free decision.

'*If anyone wants to follow me, let him deny himself*': this is the first requisite. As Peter when he denies Jesus will say: 'I do not know this man', so the followers must no longer know themselves. They must forget 'I', with its many anxieties and its petty pretensions; indeed, they must reject 'I'. They must not torment and afflict themselves. They must not make war upon themselves and defeat themselves so as to bring to birth their more noble spiritual or moral selves. Rather, they must regard the Son of Man and him alone, all their self-experience must be wholly in him and no longer in themselves. Then they will no longer realize themselves. Then they will realize in themselves and in their lives the Son of Man and his humanity. When anyone takes upon himself Christ's messianic suffering, which redeemed the world, he will stop going in circles around his own 'I', whether that came from pride or from bewilderment. Thus, denying oneself to follow Jesus has nothing to do with masochistic self-defeat. That goes without saying.

'*And let him take his cross upon himself*':

This is the second, the fulfilling requisite of the new life. It presupposes that the denial of self has been a free choice. It does not make of that self-denial an inner conflict of soul, but a reality in life's sufferings. It must be clearly stated that 'cross' is not here a symbol of any one kind of pain or other. To take one's cross upon oneself means, literally, to accept a sentence of death and to carry the instrument of one's execution, as Jesus carried his to Golgotha. Whoever follows the Son of Man condemns his inhuman, anxious, overweening 'I' to death. He receives his new life from the freedom of the Son of Man. He has as it were put his death behind him, and now confronts life with no reservations. So he is prepared for the sufferings of the world, and for the world's redemption from suffering, through his acceptance.

Nor does 'cross' here allude to the discomforts of natural existence, but to the outward and inward sufferings which arise from the following of the Son of Man in an inhuman world, and which are inescapable. These sufferings are not for us to choose or to devise. Whoever follows the Son of Man is promised no better fate here than was Jesus himself.

16

Following the way of the cross is sharing Christ's Passion in the world (Dietrich Bonhoeffer). This Passion is here called 'cross'. That points to Golgotha. But it says expressly: 'Let him take *his cross* upon himself'. No-one can, no-one is supposed to carry Christ's Cross. Every man should carry his own cross. No-one can, no-one should offer himself for the sins of the world, and endure that rejection out of which the world's reconciliation was made. That was for Jesus alone. That was his term of suffering. The burden of the world lay upon him. Of none of his followers is it expected that he will carry the world's burden once again and repeat Golgotha. Jesus the Son of Man went alone through this anguish. That is why his sufferings can be called *sufferings for reconciliation*. Following him in suffering is a *liberating suffering*, because of that unique suffering of atonement. For each man the term of the suffering which he will find in his life and carry with his strength is measured out. It lies there, all ready in the story of his life, waiting to be accepted and borne.

The 'cross' unites Jesus and his followers, and it also differentiates them. Jesus dies in complete solitude. He descends alone into the hell of abandonment by God. Nothing of this solitude and hell is spared to his followers. They too know desolation and the God who is far off. But they walk through suffering by his side and in his company. 'He tears his way through death, through the world, through sin, through violence, he tears his way through hell, and I am always his companion', Paul Gerhardt has written. Death, world, sin, violence, hell — they are all the same. But in the midst of them those who follow find the Son of Man, who has gone before them and has prepared their way. That is why a follower goes into the darkness of suffering with the certainty that as a 'companion' of the Son of Man he will be borne along. In Christ's company he will find both suffering and life, both solitude and company, both torment and certainty, both hell and heaven. If we listen to the testimony of the Christian martyrs, their experiences tell us of both one and the other. They were alone, and found in Christ's solitude their community with God. They suffered in soul and body, and found in Christ's sufferings God's strength. They experienced the depths of abandonment by God, and found it in Christ's unequivocal certainity of God.

Whoever follows Jesus in suffering and takes his own cross upon himself finds God in his life.

4

The Measure of the Passion

———————◆◆———————

Over Jesus's announcement of his sufferings and his call to follow him there lies a mystery.

On the one hand, we are commonly acquainted with suffering: poverty, hunger, sickness, exploitation, oppression, alienation and uncertainty. It seizes upon us and torments us. But on the other hand we are seeking a life without suffering, without poverty, hunger, sickness, without exploitation, oppression, alienation and uncertainty.

Therefore we should prefer a third course, to banish suffering from the world, or, at least, to reduce it to what can be escaped.

Jesus for his part is clearly reckoning with a suffering which will be conquered only if he will accept it and bear it. He is reckoning with an abandonment by God which will be conquered only if he takes it upon himself. He is reckoning with a rejection which will be transformed only if he will assent to it. The suffering for himself and his followers of which he speaks must be endured and borne if it is to pass. Either the world must bear it, and break under it because it cannot be borne by the world, or else it will fall upon God's Son of Man, and will, all of it, become his one suffering, so that the world can live (Bonhoeffer). This suffering will not be conquered through being borne in ignorance. It will not be conquered through being dismissed. It will not be conquered through being thrust upon others. This suffering will be borne through acceptance. Because the Son of Man bears it, it becomes bearable.

One might be tempted to ask whether the suffering which is in the world and oppresses mankind has at all diminished, because men from the very beginning have striven against it? If that were so, we should have reason for optimism, for hoping that in the future we should go on, always forcing suffering to retreat, always making life happier. It is true that from time to time we succeed in our battle against hunger, plague, oppression and war. But it may be that most often all that we achieve is the postponement of suffering's great burden. We conquer our own hunger, and let others starve for us. We become immune to ancient plagues, and prone to the sicknesses of civilization. All the time we lay the burdens of suffering on other men, or put them off for ourselves to another day, and so we think that we have overcome them. To think this is to be deluded and deceived.

Scripture here shows us that Jesus stood under a divine command, and he himself calls men to follow him and to accept suffering. He does not conquer suffering by setting it aside, but by accepting it freely, by taking it upon himself in our place. The God whom we can recognize in this Son of Man is a God who knows suffering, and who takes upon himself the sufferings of the world in his love, so that mankind may live. God's Son of Man bears the Cross, he bears us with our hostilities, and in the midst of our battle, by his bearing, he makes our reconciliation. Whoever follows him bears his own part of the sufferings which oppress the world. He does not bear this by his own strength. He bears it with Christ's strength, which is mighty in its weakness. But man does bear his part. No longer does he unload his sufferings upon others. Rather, he takes other men's suffering upon himself and carries it for them. In this way he too in his own walk of life spreads peace in the midst of strife. Plainly, this is the apostle's thought in his letter to the Colossians (1:24): 'I rejoice in my sufferings, that I suffer for you, and that I complete in my flesh what is still wanting of the sufferings of Christ for his body which is the Church'.

The suffering which is imposed upon the world cannot be carried out in ignorance. It cannot be thrust upon others. Either way will add to it. It must be borne if it is to be overcome. Scripture shows us Jesus entering upon his death so as to bear it. Through his suffering and his death it has become bearable for us. And as it becomes bearable, it has already been overcome and turned into joy. Jesus calls 'the people and the disciples' to follow him, so that each one will take his own cross and his own portion of that suffering upon himself, and carry out what has been imposed upon the world, and through his carrying spread abroad the joy of the kingdom on earth of the Son of Man.

II

Messianic History
as the Story of the Passion

Johann Baptist Metz

Mark (8:31 — 38) (2)

In the following meditation we attempt to approach and grasp what may be considered as the chief interest of the Gospel according to Mark, and what can be seen with special clarity in our extract (8:31— 38): our search for the Messias's secret, and, in particular, our search to establish, through the history of the Passion, the history of the Messias. We have tried to approach this question by meditating upon three points of view:

1. Verses 31 — 33: Peter's misunderstanding, or 'Against the Victors'.
2. Verses 34 — 38: Consequences or 'Political Life of Suffering between the Front Lines' ('Galilee 1973').
3. The Passion never discussed, or 'The Passion of the Son of Man and the nameless history of the world's sufferings'!

1

Peter's misunderstanding, or 'Against the Victors'.

———————————◆————————————

"And he began to teach them: "The Son of Man must suffer many things, and be rejected by the elders, the high priests and the scribes, and be put to death, and after three days rise again". He said this to them openly; but Peter took him on one side and began to reprehend him. But he turned around and looked at his disciples and reprehended Peter and said: "Go back and leave me, you Satan, for you are not thinking God's thoughts but men's thoughts' ".

'The Son of Man must suffer many things . . .' Jesus, Mark assures us, says this 'openly': Messianic history is no story of success leading on to success, but a history of suffering, of rejection and of decline; there can be no talk of salvation and of life except by and through that history. The contradiction appears at once: 'Peter took him on one side and began to reprehend him'. Fortunately, the exegetes assure us that this passage is not a later addition written out of animosity towards Peter; for it is plain that here he is speaking and reasoning for us all, in all our names. Jesus confirms this for him: 'you are thinking men's thoughts'. 'Men's thoughts' — thoughts which are not extravagant, arrogant, contemptible, but quite simply those thoughts which occur to men oppressed and humiliated by the history of their own sufferings. If they had any thought of salvation, how could they think of it except as Peter did? How could they think except in terms of human victory? And, thinking so, they will never be able to accept this saying, again and again they will come into conflict with it, and, in the end, they will only accept its incomprehensible promises as contradicting its literal sense. Jesus's sharp reproof, it is clear, is not directed at Peter alone; it is true that it is he who will deny the Man of Sorrows, but the other disciples, witnessing now this contention between Jesus and Peter, will fall asleep or run away as the Passion story advances towards its climax. And the Church, proceeding from the same incomprehension, will fail again and again to understand. For the Church this episode in Mark is related, above else, so that as she recounts and remembers the Messianic story she will not distort it into a tale of human victory, will not draw false parallels with the conquerors of history, will not display her little faith by telling this as a merely earthly event, without recalling as completely as she should that she alone is called to follow one who was conquered, for whom the verdict of 'man's thoughts' will always be: Woe to him!.

Jesus calls Peter 'Satan', and stresses remorselessly how fatal, how ineradicable this misunderstanding is. And as we read this first prophesy by Christ of his Passion, as we are confronted with the suffering, dying, conquered Mes-

sias we are impelled to clear up our own misunder-
standings, to revise our own point of view.

'The Son of Man must suffer many things . . .' This
account of the Passion of the Messias repels us more and
more, we suspect it more and more as myth. More and
more, because we are hampered by our general lack of
understanding for suffering, our deep-seated callousness
towards suffering, our dreadful fear of being moved by
suffering. Fed on the illusion of a society which can be
wholly free of suffering, we find ourselves in flight from it.
And the more we strive for total emancipation as our
ideal, the less shall we wish to hear of suffering; we shall
not recognize it except as the dead prehistory of our
freedom's triumph. In social and political Utopias, it is
simple to lump the history of the Passion together with all
the other stories of an oppressive social order which is
now obsolete; but such a vision of the human race, freed
of its heritage and of its class-structure, is by no means the
vision of a situation wholly free of suffering, whether or
not it envisages an apotheosis of total banality. For us to
take one step following the suffering Son of Man, we must
first break free from the silent decree of our 'progressive'
societies which forbids us to suffer, and we must do this,
not by some abstract counter-cult of suffering, but so as to
make ourselves capable, through our own ability to suffer,
of suffering for the sorrows of others and in this way of
drawing close to the mystery of the suffering of the Man of
Sorrows. We can achieve advances in technology, in
civilization without this ability to suffer; but when we are

concerned with truth and with freedom, without it we cannot progress, nor shall we come a single pace closer to the Son of Man.

'The Son of Man must suffer many things'. The prophesy of the Passion becomes more exact and intense: 'The Son of Man will be rejected and killed'. A Messias among the dead! Salvation in the abyss: 'He descended into hell'. The stumbling-block has been perfected, the suspicions of mythology are once and for all confirmed! Because, in the name of progress and enlightenment and emancipation, we cannot, we must not concern ourselves with the kingdom of the dead. Let the dead bury the dead! It is true that we shall still know pain, mourning, melancholy and the often wordless sufferings over the unconsoled sorrows of the past, over the sufferings of the dead. But stronger than this, it would seem, is our fear of any contact whatever with death, our lack of feeling for the dead, the banality of our depressions and the transience of our unhappy consciousness. They have all become the undergrowth of our temporal expectations and hopes, the secret principles on which we have constructed our own salvation history, which is in the end a history of success and of conquerors. In that history, as in nature, the law of the stronger rules, and the principle of selection is that of survival and tenacity. That history strides across the prostrate corpses of the condemned multitude, the dead; and in it there rules an objective cynicism with regard to past suffering, with regard to the freedom of the dead themselves: Woe to the conquered! Our silence during the epoch of the war in Vietnam was bad enough; but what seems to me worse, more sinister, more inhuman, is our silence since then, the way in which we have accepted the dead, the butchered, the destroyed by fire, the acres of ruins as the order of the day. Forgotten! Who is still seeking for friends, for brothers among these dead? And where do such questions lead us? Society knows well how to protect itself from them; the psychiatrist is lying in wait for those who persist in asking them. In our progressive societies they are in operation everywhere, the edicts against melancholy, against mourning; whether openly or in secret, they have been decreed by the facile optimism of the conquerors, of the survivors.

Concern for the dead? A Messias among the dead? Just let the dead bury their dead! But the problem of how to forget and obliterate the dead, once their life is over, is not in essence a human problem. To do that would be to forget and to expunge our past sufferings, to assent, supinely, to that suffering's lack of sense. Nor will any joy for our children recompense the sorrows of our fathers, no social progress can lay healing hands on the injustices which the dead endured. If we assent too long to the senselessness of death and of the dead, we shall in the end have nothing to offer the living but used-up secrets. It is not only the growth of our economic potentiality which is limited, as people today insist to us; the potentiality of our thinking seems also to be limited, and it is as if our reserves were dwindling, as if there were the danger that

the big words with which we made our own history —
'freedom', 'emancipation', 'justice', 'happiness' — in the
end will have no sense which has not been exhausted and
dispersed.

In such a situation it will be well for us to listen more
attentively than Peter did as Jesus foretells his Passion. It
will be well if we hear with care and with assent how it
ends: 'And He will rise again on the third day'. These are
only a few words, and it would be easy to miss them; but
they are not added merely to appease us. They point to
the victory of the Son of Man over death, they speak of a
victory, won for the oppressed, for the conquered, for
those who have been silenced and forgotten in death;
they are spoken in defiance of our human history of
conquests. They are said not from the point of view of
those who have survived, but of those who have gone
under as the play of this world has been acted out: God is
always on the side of the weak. They are full of protest
against every attempt to reduce by half life's livingness,
what we have here called its 'sense', and to reserve it
exclusively for those yet to come, for those who will
survive, for the final victors, as it were, of our history. In
the suffering and slain Messias this livingness belongs to
the very dead, and in them to us all.

2

Consequences or 'Political Life of Suffering between the Front Lines' (Galilee 1973)

————————•◆•————————

'And he called the people to him together with his disciples, and said to them: "If anyone wishes to follow after me, let him deny himself and take his cross upon him, and follow me. For whoever wishes to save his life will lose it; but whoever loses his life for the sake of me and of the Gospel will save it. For what will it help a man to gain the whole world and forfeit his life? For what could a man pay as a price for his life? For whoever is ashamed of me and my words in this adulterous and sinful generation, the Son of Man will be ashamed of him, when he comes in the glory of his Father with the holy angels".'

I should like to illumine the purport of this collection of what are called 'imitation sayings' by recounting them in the light of the situation in which Mark (according to the opinion of representative exegetes) composed his Gospel, the situation in Galilee at the time of the Roman wars of conquest. Perhaps this plan will not exhaust all significance of the imitation sayings, but it will make plain one which is central and indispensable.

In Galilee in the years between 66 and 70 AD in the

33

period immediately before the destruction of Jerusalem in the year 70, the land was overshadowed by war. There were Roman troops everywhere. The Jewish Zealots were meeting the superior power of the Roman conquerors with embittered resistance. In single villages of the countryside small groups of Christians had formed. Most of them were drawn from the earlier community in Jerusalem. Galilee, a land torn apart, divided by its hatreds, unhappy, was for them the landscape of the Parousia, the country to which the Son of Man would return. Their faith in the Messias who had come, their hope that he would come again, drove them out of their concealment, denied them their reticence and their fearful silence, as they looked upon the fiery land of their hopes. They went out upon the roads to proclaim his salvation and his peace, 'not to be ashamed of his words'. This drew them between all that established front lines, into the cross fire of enemies. They were not permitted political innocence. They were caught between systems, between the Zealots' system of a political religion and the Romans' system of an imperial state religion. What they had to say against this was little and ineffective. Their way of the Cross could be foreseen, their destruction could be calculated. Their will to follow Christ led them to a political life of suffering between the front lines. They set off, and the words of Jesus sounded in their ear like a command to a mission: 'If anyone wants to follow after me let him deny himself and take his cross upon him, and follow me, for whoever wishes to save his life will lose it; but whoever loses his life for the sake of me and of the

Gospel will save it . . . For whoever is ashamed of me and of my words in this adulterous and sinful generation, the Son of Man will be ashamed of him, when he comes in the glory of his Father with the holy angels'.

Galilee 1973. Many of our Christian illusions are shattered. Christianity's great diminution has begun. Christianity, we hear them say, is now not even a private matter. The great, reassuring coalitions are breaking up. There are no longer Christian 'systems', with their automatic guarantees of shelter and their grants to the Church of the plentitude of powers of a quasi-state. Where are we to be led if we are not ashamed of the words of the Son of Man? Where are we to be led by imitating Christ? Into the ghetto? Behind locked doors, imitating him, more or less, when we are alone, keeping frightened silence before the open hatred and enmity of the world, the land of his Parousia? Or between the systems, into a political life of suffering between the front lines?

Camus remarks to the effect that there have always been lions and martyrs, but that they have always been far outnumbered by the spectators, those on the benches. But it is the possibility of neutrality which is decreasing; this is where resources are dwindling and the distant hills are disappearing. The front line is everywhere, and it becomes harder all the time to find shelter under Christian systems, to ally ourselves as Christians with any social idealogy. If we imitate Christ, if we hope for his Parousia, where does that lead us? The systems which today make trial of our fidelty and our hope have grown more tolerant, but more embracing, more impermeable. There is always a place in them for Christian religion — to absorb painful disillusions, to neutralize uncomprehended fears, to silence dangerous recollections and ungovernable hopes. But when Christian religion rejects the role assigned to it, quickly it perceives its impotence, and then very often turns aside into the mysticism of a great refusal, keeping silent in every social context. But such withdrawal will lead fast to the well-established playgrounds of the religious underworld, where entertainment is provided for society. Where, then, will following Christ lead us to — today?

Jesus was neither a fool nor a rebel. But, plainly, he could easily be mistaken for one or the other: Herod mocked him as a fool, and his countrymen handed him over as a rebel to be crucified. Whoever follows him, whoever is not ashamed of his words must reckon with the likelihood of falling victim to this mistake, and so of landing between all the front lines — again and again, more and more. Galilee 1973.

3

The Passion never discussed, or 'The Passion of the Son of Man and the nameless history of the world's sufferings'.

Finally we must speak, briefly at least, of something which our text does not make explicit, of that suffering which remains unmentioned, the nameless history of the world's sufferings: of the many crosses beside the one Cross, of the countless, nameless perishings, of the speechless, stifled sufferings, of the massacred children from Herod's days to Auschwitz and Vietnam.

Here our text gives us cause for disquiet, for disquiet over that suffering which is not specifically named in the Passion story of the Son of Man and in the Passion story of his imitators. People will say that closer scrutiny will show that this nameless suffering is not excluded and that there are texts in which our attention is drawn precisely to it. That is so. Yet the practical Bible-exposition which we have used in the history of Christianity and of the Church, the practiced exegesis of the Passion of Jesus and of those who have followed him must make us cautious in this matter. Have we not too much interiorized his sufferings and our own? Have we, through personalizing the

37

suffering in the earthly Son of Man and those who have followed him, not created vast spaces, spaces of a nameless suffering? And have we not underestimated this suffering's reward, not set it far to low? Have we not, confronted by the suffering, become frightenly apathetic and indifferent? As if this suffering could be considered as a purely earthly element and as if we could regard ourselves, opposed to it, as the great and final victors? As if this suffering had no expiatory powers, as if we did not all live in its debt? How otherwise can that Passion history be understood which we Christians have through the centuries (in the context of our world and culture) offered to the Jewish people? If not before, we have known at least since Auschwitz that we Christians too after such horrors can only call upon God's name without hypocrisy because there are those, more than can be counted or named, who named him and called upon him in those horrors, the most of them Jews. Christians live in the debt of a nameless suffering which cannot be identified as Christian; this universality of suffering should not go unmentioned here.

We do not wish by this to do anything to cheapen that suffering; nothing should be comprehended in it, no claims should be made for it, if that is not legitimate. One wishes only to signal the depths and the breadth, often exaggerated, often minimized, of that story of suffering which we call the history of the Passion of the Son of Man. Is it really a coincidence that in hardly any other realm do the exegetes find sich difficulties as in delineating and identifying exactly that 'Son of Man'? 'The Son of Man must suffer many things . . .' The statements about the subject of this suffering remain vague and ambiguous. The history of his Passion has not yet reached its conclusion. Anyone who rejects this, in the name of theological precision or sober orthodox, as inferior Passion-mysticism, has hardly understood. Only when we Christians give ear to the dark prophesy of the nameless, unrecognized, misunderstood and misprized Passion do we hear aright the message of his suffering. A well-known judgment saying from the New Testament makes that very clear: 'Lord, when did we ever see you suffering . . . ?' (Matthew 25:31 — 46).